THE
JUST ONE LOOK
METHOD

Complete Instructions

Just One Look Press

THE JUST ONE LOOK METHOD

Complete Instructions

ISBN: 978-0-9718246-3-8 (paperback)
Library of Congress Control Number: 2018908010

ASIN: B07B4XG22J (Kindle ebook)

Edited by Carla Sherman

Front cover image: Simon Matzinger
Book design: Carla Sherman

Just One Look Press
201 E. Ojai Avenue, 1566
Ojai, California 93023
United States of America

Phone: +1 (805) 649-1600
info@justonelook.org

Visit www.JustOneLook.org

Printed and bound in the United States of America.
First published in March 2018. Revised and updated on May 5, 2019.

Contents

Welcome to Just One Look

The Just One Look Method is an extremely simple approach to mental misery unlike anything you have ever tried. It will rid you of the root cause of your dissatisfaction with life and the painful yearning for peace and fulfillment that seems never to be fully satisfied.

The Just One Look Method is the result of twenty years of experience working with people all around the world who have seen their relationship with their own lives change dramatically for the better.

The Just One Look Method
Complete Instructions

Step One: Look at Yourself

Sit down, close your eyes, and just breathe for a little while. When you feel relaxed, put your attention on the sensation of your tongue resting in your mouth and focus on that sensation for a minute or so.

After a while, move your attention to the feeling of your feet resting on the floor and focus on that sensation for a minute.

After a minute or so, place the focus of your attention on the air passing in and out of your nose and stay with that sensation for a minute.

Now, in the same way that you directed your attention to the feeling of your tongue, your feet, and your breath, direct your attention inward, looking for the faint sensation of what it *feels* like to be you—what you would call *me.*

What you are looking for here is the simple *me-ness* of you; you are *not* looking for the thoughts or the emotions that rise and fall within you or any ideas about your nature that you have heard or read about.

You are *here.* You cannot deny that you exist. What makes

you certain that you exist? What makes it impossible for you to deny that you are here?

Another effective way to get a glimpse of what it feels like to be you is to use a childhood memory.

To begin, just sit back and relax for a moment.

Close your eyes and just watch your breath for a little while. Breathe in... Breathe out... Focus your attention on the sensation of the air coming in and out of your nose. Do this for about one minute.

Now try to bring to mind a memory of an event from your childhood. It does not need to be anything special. For John, it was the memory of coming out of an afternoon matinee on a hot summer day in New Jersey, when he was eight years old.

Just relax, and wait for a memory to appear. When a vivid memory appears, see whether you are remembering it as if you were watching a movie, watching yourself as a character in the movie, as the memory unfolds in your mind. If you are, try now to go inside the scene, to get the feel of it.

When you get the memory in mind and sink into the feel of it, try to see *what it felt like to be you then*, experiencing it all.

Now, move your attention one more time—this time to

what it feels like to be you now.

This simple act of inward looking at your *me-ness,* the sensation that you would call *me,* automatically and instantaneously puts an end to the background murmur of anxiety, distrust, and dissatisfaction that is the experience of life for most of us.

If it is done right, just one look at yourself is enough but, since directing our attention inward is something we are not accustomed to doing, it may be hard to tell if you have done it right. We advise you to continue trying to have the experience of your *me-ness* directly, even if just for a moment, whenever you feel the desire to do so. Do it until you are satisfied. It is a safe place to put your attention.

In time, as you begin to see the changes unfold in your mind, you will simply lose interest in doing the act of Looking at Yourself since, in fact, you are never *not* here.

Step Two: Self-Directed Attention Exercise

After looking at yourself for the first time, you may experience relief, lightness, and a sense that all is well for a few days, weeks, or even months. That is what we call the "honeymoon period." Then, there may be a period of confusion and psychological difficulty in which old patterns of thought and behavior may reappear.

You do not have to do anything to kill those diseased psychological mechanisms off because the only way that they live is through *the energy you give them by attending to them.* Just pay them no mind and they will die of starvation.

We think of this time of confusion as the period of recovery from a psychological autoimmune disease, and this recovery can be truly miserable.

The best way to get through this difficult time is to start a daily practice of the Self-Directed Attention Exercise as explained below. Our purpose with this exercise is to cultivate a very useful skill that will help you develop self-reliance during the difficult period that follows the collapse of the atmosphere of fear that has shaped every aspect and psychological mechanism of your mind.

As you will see, the instructions for the Self-Directed Attention Exercise are very simple but, since even the simplest instructions can be misunderstood because of all the ideas and concepts that we all carry around with us, it is best to put aside everything you know for a while and focus on simply following the instructions.

The most effective way to develop self-reliance is the training of your ability to direct and focus your attention at will. This exercise will strengthen your ability to focus attention on a single object, ignoring everything else that may be going on in your mind, as a means to develop your natural skillfulness in the intelligent use of this power.

In the beginning, this exercise is hard to do for everybody, but only because we are not used to doing it. Most of the time, we do not even know that we can control our attention, but we promise you: *you can do it.*

Sit down, close your eyes, and just focus on the sensation of the air as it goes in and out of your nose. Spend ten minutes just trying to feel that sensation. You may notice that the sensation is cooler as it passes through the nostrils coming into the body and warmer on its way out of the body. It is that feeling, that sensation in your nostrils that you will pay attention to and focus on.

You may want to do just that the first time. If it seems to you that you cannot feel the sensation of the breath in your nostrils, continue trying. Focus your attention on the tip of your nose. In time, you will start being able to feel it.

Next time, try counting the outbreaths. Try to create a tight focus on the sensation of the breath coming in and out of the nose. At the end of every outbreath, count mentally: one, two, three... The first outbreath is one, the second outbreath is two, and so forth. Until you get to ten. If you get to ten, start over from one.

When you notice that your attention has been hijacked and you are paying attention to something other than the sensation of your breath in your nostrils—a physical sensation, a train of thought, a sound, an itch, or something crossing your field of vision—simply move your attention back to the sensation of the breath in your nostrils and start counting again from one. And if you get to ten, start over from one.

For instance, you may find yourself thinking that this exercise is stupid and you are never going to get it; or that it is too easy, and what is the point of doing it anyway? When you notice that you are thinking and not doing the exercise, stop. Do not criticize yourself, do not tell yourself you cannot do it, etc. Stop right there and immediately direct your attention to the sensation of your breath and start counting again from one.

This is completely normal. Do not be discouraged. Do not push yourself too hard. Be patient with yourself. Start counting your breaths from one every time you get distracted. Keep trying; do not give up. Even if you stop at two or three and start over every time, the work is being done. Remember, the goal of this exercise is not to get to a point where you can count to high numbers or even count up to ten. The point is to notice when you have moved away from the focus point (the breath) and then deliberately *choose* to pay attention to the sensation of the breath in your nose again. It is this *conscious act of intentionally directing your attention* that counts. You must do this exercise as you would lift weights or do push-ups to develop and strengthen your muscles. Even if you can only count to one or two before noticing that you were distracted, the work is being done.

If you find yourself counting up to very high numbers without being distracted, pay closer attention. It is very easy to go on automatic pilot and keep counting even though your attention is divided. Whenever you cannot tell if you were distracted or not, stop and start over from one. Pay attention. Do not be discouraged. Persist.

Do this exercise for only ten minutes at a time, once or twice a day. For instance, you can do it when you wake up and before you go to sleep. Set a timer so you will know when the time is over.

It is very important *not* to make any attempt to control the way the breathing is happening. If you experience hyperventilation when doing the Self-Directed Attention Exercise, it is possible that you are trying to manage your breathing. You may be unconsciously trying to accelerate it, slow it down, make it kind of rhythmic, or trying to make it remain in compliance with your counting speed. This may lead to hyperventilation and even raise your blood pressure. You may experience heart palpitations.

To overcome this problem, let the focus of your attention rest on the sensation in your nose. You can be completely focused on the sensation and relaxed at the same time. Do not attempt to control your breathing. Just watch the inbreaths and the outbreaths as they happen, without any effort to make them regular or irregular or to change them in any way. Most often, when we start paying attention to our breathing, it gets more prominent and regular and even deeper. The key is to watch your natural breath, as it would happen without you watching it.

Paying attention to the airflow as it goes through your nostrils is the best way to do this. Using this technique, instead of paying attention to the movement of your chest or abdomen as you breathe, naturally makes your breathing more shallow.

Try not to obsess over this exercise. It is not about trying to pay attention to your breath *all the time*, or devoting yourself to any other such nonsense. Your only purpose with this exercise is to develop *your ability to direct your attention where you want it to go.*

The results will start to appear in time. It will not take long before you start to see the real benefits of this exercise in your life. After some time of practice, if you pay attention, you will notice that now there is a slight space between you and your thoughts and feeling states. Just enough space for you to see them for what they are. They are all just thoughts. They are not you. You can look at them, and you can decline to give your attention to them. In time, that space will grow.

To benefit fully from this exercise, you must first look at yourself as explained in Step One. If you are not sure that you were able to follow the instructions, do not hesitate to ask for help. You can find help and support by joining our online meetings, by having a private session with us, and by posting your questions in the Just One Look Forum.

In the beginning, it may seem that this exercise is the hardest thing you have ever tried to do, but it is really worth it and we guarantee you will not regret doing it. It is not a quick fix but, if you do the work, you will succeed.

You may go through a difficult period, but that will pass. Some people find it useful to write down the changes they notice in their behavior. If you are so inclined, keeping a diary can help you track and understand your progress.

Using Self-Directed Attention in Daily Life

After practicing the Self-Directed Attention Exercise for a while, start using your attention to help the healing of your mind.

During the recovery period, while your mind is reconstituting itself from a new ground of sanity, disturbing thoughts may still appear and old patterns of reaction may be triggered by certain circumstances.

Many thoughts will come to you, trying to distract you from this work. Thoughts of doubt, defeatism, hopelessness, fear, anger, etc. Any thought that does not offer a practical solution to a problem in the moment is irrelevant *in the moment.* It is safe to ignore it by moving your attention away from it.

Move your attention away from the disturbing thought and place it on the feeling of your breath as you learned with the practice of the Self-Directed Attention Exercise. At this stage, you do not need to count the breaths anymore. Just move your attention away from the thought and place it on the sensation of the breath in your nostrils.

A disturbing thought may be connected to a physical

sensation. This intentional movement of attention can also help with disturbing physical sensations. Move your attention to the sensation and experience it directly, without naming it or trying to get rid of it. Just feel it completely for as long as you can.

You can alternate between directing your attention to the sensation of the breath in your nostrils and directing your attention to the disturbing sensation in your body.

It is often the case that a person will do the act of Looking at Yourself, not notice immediate results, then "forget" all about it. We assure you, the process will continue subconsciously, even if you think that the method is not working for you.

A regular practice of the Self-Directed Attention Exercise will enable you to have more control of your attention and you will be more aware of the changes that are happening in your mind.

If you are not aware of what is happening to you, it is very likely that you will face mental, and sometimes physical, difficulties all alone. It is very important to keep in touch, to connect with others who are going through the same process. Our community is spread around the world. Connecting with others who can understand what you are going through brings encouragement and confirmation.

Please let us know how this process unfolds for you. Since there are many people who write asking for help, it is best to post your reports and questions in the Just One Look Forum. We read every post and reply when needed. There are also many people in the forum who have gone through this process and will be able to help you. Your reports and questions will help others too.

Understanding the Fear of Life

The fear of life is the first cause of all our purely psychological difficulties. The fear of life is a silent and false assumption that life is untrustworthy and dangerous and it runs in the background of all experience.

Now, strictly speaking, there is no requirement that you understand the cause of your mental misery to rid yourself of it and, conversely, mere understanding of the cause will not free you of it. Nevertheless, a clear understanding of the actual cause of your mental misery, although not required, vastly simplifies and mitigates the experience of regeneration that often follows that first look at yourself.

The act of Looking at Yourself eradicates the fear of life and it requires no understanding, belief, or preconditions of any kind. But seeing clearly the actual cause of your mental suffering is very useful because it reveals that nothing you have done based on the assumption that your psychology is the problem has ever given you any permanent relief.

Although our understanding of how the psychology works

in service to the fear of life has become much clearer in recent times, that insight is not new. Many others throughout the ages have come to understand the nature of the mind, and the psychological mechanisms that comprise the mind, with great clarity and in detail but, to our knowledge, no one has found any fundamental and permanent fix for its madness.

Because of the dominance that the foundation of fear and distrust holds over the mind and its mechanisms—and despite the dismal history of consistent failure to provide decisive and permanent relief—it has been all but impossible for even those with the greatest clarity and maturity of understanding to suspect that there might be some *event* or *condition* appearing prior to the development of the psychology that sets the context within which the mind takes form in such a way as to require the mind to distrust life itself as a matter of existential significance and import.

Religion sees more clearly the *hiddenness* of the actual cause of our pain, and has proposed a variety of supernatural explanations such as original sin, reincarnation, satanic forces, and the like, to explain the mind's insane tendency to suffer. Unfortunately, the religious approaches have had no greater success than the psychological ones in ridding us of this curse.

Still, we continue to pursue solutions based on false insights and broken understandings, which create the illusion that the mind—that is to say, the ensemble of psychological mechanisms—is to blame for all the trouble that stifles and ruins the experience of being alive as a human being. Once that false assumption is firmly seated, even the clearest and truest among us are blocked from considering any way out other than religion, philosophy, immersion in the ancient wisdom teachings, or psychotherapeutic practices aimed at taming psychological mechanisms that are actually *untamable*.

We are told, with all the best intentions, that we must either reform the mind by gaining understanding of what we *should* think and feel, and cleanse it with practices designed to clarify and give power to our understandings, or seek supernatural forces that will free us from the mind's grip. As a last resort, many of the wisdom teachings advise us to try to destroy it.

Please stop here for a moment or two, if you will, and try to take in what we have just suggested, without regard for whatever thoughts may be present in your mind about it all. Consider for a moment the possibility that the thoughts, assumptions, and mechanisms of understanding that comprise your mind may be rooted in a *profoundly erroneous idea about you and your life.*

Can you see that, if what we say is true, then no one is to blame for any of it? Neither you, nor the mind, nor even the fear, really. After all, the fear of life struck of its own accord, accidentally, through the fault of no one.

If you look at yourself in the manner we suggest, the fear of life will go whether you understand it or not, but we believe that understanding the actual cause of the problem for which the Looking provides a cure will profoundly affect the course of recovery from the consequences of a life crippled by fear.

The fear of life comes upon almost all of us accidentally at birth, when the shock and violence of our arrival sets the context within which our entire psychology—all of our understandings, all of our bedrock assumptions, our likes and dislikes, and our sense of identity—will take form. The fear of life is the cause of all human aggression and self-destructive behavior.

The fear of life is a psychological autoimmune disease. It seeks to protect us from the perceived danger of being alive by holding life itself at arm's length. It warps the lens of personal psychology through which we perceive the meaning, validity, and the potential effect of everything that happens to us, within us, and around us. It creates and maintains the delusion that life is not safe, that life is not to be trusted. It poisons our minds and our relationships with one another, and with the Earth itself.

All of our self-hatred and hatred of others, all of our self-defeating and aggressive habits of behavior and relationship, and all of our misery and disappointment in ourselves and in our lives spring from one simple cause, and that is the fear of life, which drives us insane.

The fear of life is not among the natural fears that we are familiar with, fears that come and go in reaction to arising events in our lives. It is a silent, false assumption that life is untrustworthy and dangerous.

The fear of life shuns all interest in or awareness of itself. The presence of that unseen assumption stains the development of the individual's entire psychological structure, and it is the source of all resistance to any efforts from forces outside of its influence to set right the individual psychology.

Along with the realization that nothing you have done based on the assumption that your psychology is the problem has ever given you any permanent relief, understanding the actual cause of the problem also gives rise to two other important insights: First, you are not responsible for the madness of your own mind; and second, you need not attend to its shenanigans as it regenerates, after the fear of life is gone.

When we see the actual cause of all the trouble, the almost worshipful relationship we usually have with thoughts and beliefs vanishes. Thoughts and ideas that previously would have been a cause of obsessive concern are then known to be of no consequence.

Therefore, although it is not necessary that you understand the fear of life and its nature to free yourself of its influence and its psychological minions, when the fear is gone and you begin to have the direct experience of life, you will find that understanding to be deeply empowering and extremely helpful.

The Soldiers of Fear

The act of Looking at Yourself cleans up the slate. It removes the fear of life that is the distorted environment in which your mind (your conditioned responses, your likes and dislikes, your understandings, etc.) has developed over time. One look at the *sense of being me* flips the switch. The reality that you are always here, and that you are not at stake in your own life, is exposed and the entire project of self-protection loses its ground of being. All this happens under the radar, in what is referred to in psychology as our *subconscious.* Most people usually cannot see this clearly while they are going through the process, but we have seen it happen over and over to hundreds of people.

Now, the tools used by that project of self-protection are the mental mechanisms that, as a group, are usually referred to as the *conditioned mind*. That is all the mind is: algorithms. Algorithms are a systematic method to achieve a variable goal with different quantitative or qualitative components. They are sets of instructions, as in a computer program, and they are strictly mechanical. It is all about "If this happens, I do this," as in "If I am having worrisome thoughts, then this means that I am still not free, so this is not working for me and I must go look somewhere else for a solution." We take those thoughts to be a true, accurate description of what is happening, and we act based on that assumption.

Once the fear of life disappears, those mental mechanisms that were contaminated by the environment of the fear of life in which they were born are still in place and they do not go away immediately. They are, after all, the actual fabric of the mind, so to speak. But with the context of the fear of life gone, those old, fearful mechanisms start fading away—most often not without a fight—as new, saner mechanisms begin taking their place. This is a long process, and it does take time.

The best way to understand clearly what is happening to you and to be able to see which, if any, of those thought patterns are actually true, healthy, and useful and which are just diseased habits of mind is to develop strong control over your attention. What keeps those thought patterns in place is the attention you give to them. You have been conditioned over your lifetime to believe that thoughts are important and that you need to pay attention to them—especially the negative, pessimistic, self-destructive, and worrisome ones.

What is impossible to see in the early stages of recovery is that those thoughts that come to tell you that "This is not working for me," or "I don't agree with the theory of the fear of life as the cause of my mental difficulties," or "I don't agree with the idea that the birth trauma is at the root of our mental problems," or "This method is the same as another method I studied before, and I already know what this is all about," are all *soldiers of fear* trying to reassert themselves, trying to maintain the status quo, fighting to stay in place and to protect you from life itself. They will fight to the death to stay in place, but you do not need to trust them blindly. The only useful thing to do is to refuse to give them your attention.

The way to develop that level of control over your attention is to practice the Self-Directed Attention Exercise as described in this book. Nothing else will do it. This is not about replacing bad thoughts with good thoughts. It is about developing focus and becoming able to decline to pay attention to useless and self-destructive thoughts. If you do not feed them by paying attention to them, they will starve to death.

When one is going through a depressive period, or a

physical disease, for example, it is very hard to practice the Self-Directed Attention Exercise. The barrage of sad, negative, pessimistic thoughts is almost irresistible and it seems impossible to decline to attend to them but, if you do the practice diligently when you are able to, that effort will build up and strengthen your control over your attention so that, when times get hard, you will have a little more control. If you just cannot do the exercise, it is totally okay to take a break for a while.

As you develop more control over what you do pay attention to and what you can simply ignore, you become more able to see clearly the relationship between thought and attention. In the first weeks, maybe months, after having done the act of Looking at Yourself, it is best to follow the instructions closely and do the practice strictly without any deviation. This will not do you any harm and it is safe to trust that, since it has worked for so many people already, it will work for you too. There is nothing to lose. And it is never too much to say it again. The Self-Directed Attention Exercise will not produce the desired results unless you have looked at yourself in the manner described in this book.

Whatever fearful and worrisome thoughts still show up trying to get your attention at any cost during the period of recovery, they are *not* the fear of life and their appearance does not mean that you are not already free of fear. Those thoughts are the remaining soldiers of fear, the servants of the perceived fearful need to protect yourself from life itself, and they keep fighting, although the war is really over the moment you successfully touch yourself with your attention.

Again, the presence of those diseased, fearful thought processes (algorithms) does not mean that you are not free of the fear of life. They are just the remnants of the fear that were left behind and they will disappear eventually no matter what you do or fail to do. But a strict and serious practice of the Self-Directed Attention Exercise will hasten their disappearance and will give you a much better understanding of how your own mind works. You will be more in control of your reactions to circumstances, and that will happen naturally, in the moment. As the diseased mental mechanisms that used to make you do stupid things fade away, what is left is your own innate intelligence, no longer contaminated by the fear of life.

That is your birthright and it is the natural state of being human.

Resources

There are many resources available free of charge on our website that will be helpful to you on your journey from fear to sanity.

The Just One Look Forum is a safe place where you can post your questions and comments and read hundreds of conversations about using The Just One Look Method and recovering from the fear of life disease.

Although this is a process that everyone has to go through on their own, you can find help and encouragement from us and from fellow lookers around the world on our website. We also offer private sessions and online meetings.

For more information, visit our website:

www.justonelook.org

Contact us

John and Carla Sherman

Just One Look Foundation

201 E. Ojai Avenue, 1566

Ojai, California 93023

United States of America

Phone: +1 (805) 649-1600

Email: info@justonelook.org

www.justonelook.org

Support our Work

The Just One Look Project is a program of the Just One Look Foundation. The program was launched officially in 2012 with the goal of bringing The Just One Look Method free of charge to everyone all around the world.

The Just One Look Foundation was established in 2000 and it is a not-for-profit, public charitable organization under Section 501(c) (3) of the United States Internal Revenue Code.

All our programs are supported entirely by donations. Donations are tax-deductible for United States residents as charitable contributions.

There are many ways you can donate to support our work. More information on how to donate to the Just One Look Foundation is available on our website. You may also contact us directly by phone, email, or mail for more information.

Other Titles by John & Carla Sherman

Our paperback books and ebooks are published by Just One Look Press and can be purchased at Amazon stores worldwide and other places that sell books.

Lookers Tell Their Stories (2017)

Just One Look, the Story (2014, 2015, 2017, 2019)

The Fear of Life and the Simple Act of Inward Looking that Snuffs It Out (2014, 2017)

Just One Look: Experience the Power of Human Consciousness to Free Itself of the Fear of Life (2011, 2014, 2017)

Look at Yourself (2010)

Meeting Ramana Maharshi, Conversations with John Sherman (2004, 2017)

About the Authors

John Sherman was born in 1942 in Camden, New Jersey. Like everyone, John spent most of his life unconsciously searching for the one perfect path out of the wilderness of human life; the one perfect idea, the one perfect thing to think, to understand, to want, to have, to believe, to become that would bring him salvation and satisfaction. The course of John's search was extreme compared to most, but the result was the same: nothing worked; nothing ever does.

Late in 1969, when he was twenty-seven years old, John discovered the idea of Social Justice and set out to become the perfect Communist revolutionary. In 1975, he joined with a small group of anarcho-communist radicals, and embarked upon a series of bank robberies, property bombings, gunfights with the police, two escapes from federal prisons and two years on the FBI's Ten Most Wanted List; all done in the name of supporting the struggles of the American worker for justice.

In January of 1976, John was shot and captured during a bank robbery; in March, during a trip to the hospital, he escaped.

In March of 1978, after two years on the run, robbing banks and organizing property bombings, John was captured by the FBI. He was tried, convicted, and sentenced to thirty years in federal prison.

In March of 1979, he escaped again from the federal prison where he was serving his sentence. He was put on the FBI's Ten Most Wanted List on April 24, 1979.

On December 17, 1981, after two years on the FBI's Ten Most Wanted list, he was captured for the last time and returned to prison.

In June of 1994, in the fifteenth year of his imprisonment, John had an overwhelming experience of awakening that took him completely by surprise. He spent more than a year and a half in the fully open awareness of spiritual awakening, which then collapsed, leaving him bereft.

John spent the rest of his time in prison trying to find something that he could do that would bring him back to the state of indifference and apathy that he had enjoyed prior to that experience. This effort unexpectedly brought him to true freedom by means of an extremely simple act of attention.

Three and a half years later, in April of 1998, he was

released on parole. Upon his release, he moved to Boulder, Colorado.

Carla Sherman (née Vilela Baptista) was born in 1961 in Rio de Janeiro, Brazil. In 1987, she earned a Bachelor of Arts degree in Romance Languages (French and Portuguese) and, in 1991, a Master of Arts degree in French Literature, both at Universidade Federal do Rio de Janeiro (UFRJ) [Federal University of Rio de Janeiro]. She taught French and French Literature at her alma mater and at Universidade Estadual do Rio de Janeiro (UERJ) [State University of Rio de Janeiro].

She worked for over twelve years as a freelance translator and conference interpreter for the Consulate General of France in Rio de Janeiro, TV Educativa (TVE), and a number of publishing houses and magazines. She also worked for over ten years as a freelance translator for Drei Marc, a subtitling company in Rio.

In July of 1997, Carla was a doctoral candidate at UFRJ, preparing her PhD dissertation in French Literature, when she came to the United States to attend a silent retreat. That was her very first time in a spiritual meeting and, on the third day, she had an overwhelming experience of awakening. She went back to Rio for a few months and then came back, this time to Boulder, Colorado. In Boulder, Carla met John Sherman. She went back to Brazil after a couple of months.

A few months later, in January of 1999, she came back to the United States, this time to California, where she ran into John again. By then, after a year and a half of spiritual awakening, everything had fallen apart, and she felt completely lost. She started looking for a way to gain back the experience of the oneness of all being. This effort led her to look at herself, although she did not know it at the time. This was the beginning of a process that eventually brought her to true freedom.

John and Carla were married in June of 1999, in San Rafael, California. In 2001, they moved to Ojai, California, where they live with their cat, Switters. Carla became an American citizen in February of 2007 and John was released from parole in August of 2007.

Since 1999, John and Carla meet with people from all walks of life to speak about the fear of life, which is what spoils human life, how that comes to pass, what gives rise to it in the first place, how it manifests in life in general, and what every person can do to be free of it once and for all.

Connect with us

FACEBOOK:

facebook.com/justonelookproject

facebook.com/justonelook

YOUTUBE:

youtube.com/justonelook

TWITTER:

twitter.com/Just_OneLook